MODELING BEHAVIOR

Tim Brunson, PhD

The International Hypnosis Research Institute, LLC

CONTENTS

INTRODUCTION

At this point you should understand the NLP Communication Model, be somewhat familiar with NLP rapport concepts, and understand the core theories of how NLP techniques work, especially in light of the more modern Advanced Neuro-Noetic Hypnosis (ANNH) concepts. In this book I am going to share with you some of the advanced modeling techniques that are typically covered in the Master Practitioner program, which is the 130 hours of training that is presented during the second year.

WHAT IS MODELING?

I want to start by defining modeling from an NLP perspective. The presumption here is that a person or organization has attained a proficiency in one particular skill or function. Please note that most expert performers are clueless as to why and how they have achieved and continually replicate their proficiency. NLP as a programming tool seeks to resolve this by teaching you how you can rapidly notice a person's sequence and how to install this in a second person or organization. The first component, which is detecting the sequence, is referred to as the Calibration Stage; the second, the Installation Stage.

CALIBRATION STAGE

The Calibration Stage is somewhat similar to a diagnostic system. Those of you who are trained in psychology or psychiatry are familiar with the Multi-axial Assessment System. A medical doctor is likewise trained in differential diagnosis. Even your car mechanic is trained to use a specific diagnostic approach in order to find out why your vehicle is not performing at its best. NLP Master Practitioners have two excellent diagnostic tools. These involve Eye Accessing Cues and the assessment of the subject's Meta Program filters.

EYE ACCESSING CUES

Eye Accessing Cues is a topic that is introduced in one of the very first Practitioner-level classes. Master Practitioner students then revisit the topic during the second year of training when it is then applied to modeling. For now, I want to start off with the basic concept.

Your eyes are hardwired into your brain. In fact, I often state that your eyes are the only part of your brain that is publicly visible. Your eye movements reflect your preconscious thought.

Recently scientists have been discussing microsaccadic eye movements, which they contend reflect your preconscious thought patterns. (Please note that I am avoiding the use of the word subconscious as that term is misused and rather unscientific.)

Microsaccadic eye movements are the miniscule

rapid jerky movements of your eyes. These movements are not what I am referring to as Eye Assessing Cues. I am mentioning them here just to validate the Grinder and Bandler original theory, which stated that eye movements can reveal preconscious thought patterns.

As the theory goes, the typical right-handed person will look a specific direction when participating in one of six functions. These are Visual Recall, Visual Construct, Auditory Recall, Auditory Construct, Kinesthetic, and Auditory Digital. I will explain each of these and the typical movement in detail. By the way, when I say that a person will look in a specific direction, I am referring to this as being from your – not their – point of view. Please note that I frequently said the word typical.

Visual Recall is a visual memory of something that happened in their past. Typically, they will look up to your right.

Visual Construct is imagining what something will look like in the future. Typically, they will look up to your left.

Auditory Recall is an auditory memory of what something sounded like or someone said in the past. Typically, they will look to your right level with their eyes.

Auditory Construct is imaging what something will sound like or someone will say in the future. Typically, they will look to your left level with their eyes.

A Kinesthetic Eye Accessing will occur when the typical person looks down to your left. This occurs when they are getting in touch with their feelings.

Auditory Digital refers to a situation when your subject is talking to themselves. Typically, when this happens, they are looking down to your right.

It is important for you to calibrate to your subject. I do this by asking a series of questions such as:

What was the color of your first car? A question like this helps your subject access their Visual Recall.

What will be the color of your next home? A question like this will help your subject access their Visual Construct.

What is the first sentence of your favorite song? This will help your subject access their Auditory Recall.

What will be the first thing that you will say to your significant other during your next conversation? This will help your subject access their Auditory Construct.

How did you feel the last time someone gave you extremely good news? This will help your subject achieve Kinesthetic accessing.

Generally, Auditory Digital is the opposite of Kinesthetic. If they look down to your left when accessing their feelings, they will almost always look down to their right when talking to themselves.

I hope that you realize that when you do this calibration it is not necessary that your subject tell you what they are thinking. Their eye movements will tell you everything that you want to know.

Note that sometimes you will observe people who constantly shift their eyes from left to right or right to left. This is called shifty eyes. This may mean that they are being untruthful, as all lies are a combination of recall and construct – or to phrase it another way all lies contain an element of fact and fiction. Don't assume that this is always the case. Sometimes a very active mind will constantly seek previously installed memories or patterns as part of their effort to rapidly understand new information.

Now I want to relate Eye Accessing Cues to modeling. Once you have calibrated to your subject find something that they are particularly proud of, such as their ability to resolve complex problems, putt a golf ball, or cook a chicken casserole. It is helpful here to use the proper notation which is: V^r, V^c, A^r, A^c, K, and A^d.

As an example, I am going to use an expert speller. Their sequence could very well be V^r, A^r, A^d, K. or just V^r to K. This means that they visually see the word, sound it out in their mind, say it to themselves, make sure that it feels correct, and then say the word out loud. A bad speller will most likely follow a much different strategy such as K, A^c.

THIS IS A RECIPE FOR FAILURE

When you are attempting to install expert performance all you must do is get your subject to follow the sequence that has been proven to work in the expert. If you notice that your speller always goes kinesthetic first – which probably means that they are panicking – get them to start by seeing the word in their head first. You will be amazed at the results.

META-PROGRAMS

Another excellent tool for calibrating to a person with excellent performance is meta-programs. Think of these as another form of psychological or personality testing. The theory here is that if you can discern how someone's personality works, then you can hopefully install these attributes in someone else.

Originally, the six major meta-program categories include preferences for overview or detail, reference system, modal properties, processing, time orientation, and sorting. I will go through each of these in more detail.

When you observe someone, try to pick up their preference for generalization or detail. Do they attempt to summarize everything, or do they wish to constantly share every little detail?

Notice whether their reference system is either internal or external. For the Myers-Briggs fans, this would be somewhat like introvert or extrovert motivational styles. When calibrating to this category of meta-programs, I attempt to discern whether they are self-motivators or require someone else to constantly pump them up emotionally.

Likewise, I attempt to notice their modal properties. Here what I am looking for is whether they are proactive or reactive. Are they a mover and a shaker or are they always reacting to the actions of others? One way of determining this is asking them what makes them happy. If their answer is that their happiness is dependent on the actions of others, then I know that they are a reactive sort of person.

A second modal meta-program is their outcome preferences. Are they always attempting to achieve something because they are turned on by the goal or are they desiring to avoid the pain of defeat? Most smokers that I see are overly reactive and have an away-from preference. Moving them from one side to the other is often all that it takes. They are shocked when I suggest that they have a choice.

How does a person process information? Are they looking for sameness or differences? This processing meta-program is simple to elicit. Just ask them why they made a certain decision. This is very similar to the match/mismatch meta-program.

In *The Basis of NLP Techniques* I talked about the importance of time orientation. This is also a meta-program, as some people will describe events or situations as near or far, past or present, recent or far in the future.

The last major meta-pattern category involves their sorting preferences. Some people are self-sorters, as they constantly relate everything in terms of themselves. They will make decisions based upon how they expect to feel and relate stories and be very clear as to how the situation made them feel. They will feel that it is very important for others to recognize them and their beliefs and values. On the other hand, another-sorter will constantly talk about how others feel and make decisions based upon what they will do for others.

The other sorting meta-programs include a class of filters that reflect a person's preferential awareness concerning people, activities, locations, things, information, etc. My late father was a date sorter, as he had an uncanny ability to give you the month and year of many of the major events in his life. Also, I previously had a secretary who could easily tell me the style of dress or apparel that she wore during just about every major event of her life.

Since Robert Dilts, PhD, and Leslie Cameron came

up with the concept of meta-programs in the early 1980's, other authors have added other ones. These include assertiveness, indifference, complacency, tolerance, power, popularity, and performance.

When attempting to calibrate to someone's meta-programs, it is a matter of developing a checklist and observing and listening. Master Practitioner students are required to do this with numerous people. During that phase of my training rarely did I have a visitor to my office or a caller on the telephone without me respectfully and subtly simultaneously completing my Meta-Program checklist.

When it comes to discerning mastery and seeking to model behavior, hopefully you will pick up on the fact that expert performers almost always display specific meta-programs. For instance, when hiring a staff member for the Institute, there are certain attributes that I seek. Being a proactive, other sorting, future oriented individual is much preferable than a reactive, mismatching, past oriented, self-sorter. Additionally, in order to overcome one of my weaknesses, I tend to prefer someone that focuses on details and specificity.

Once you determine the preferred meta-programs, installing them is your next step. This is often called coaching. As previously mentioned, non-smokers tend to have a completely different set of meta-programs than smokers. By pointing this out in an appropriately tactful way, you can help them change. Likewise, should you notice that a star athlete has a specific set of meta-programs, again, it is the role of the coach to move the want-a-be star athlete in the right direction by encouraging them to change their meta-program filters toward a set that is more conducive with the desired performance.

I want to make one last comment about meta-programs. It is vital that you understand the ecology of any proposed meta-program change. Remember that any filter change will have a much more pervasive impact than you may have intended. Changing someone's sorting patterns or outcome preferences may be very difficult and may garner negative reactions in others. Therefore, once you suggest that a subject try a new meta-program on for size, you should assess the results that occur. As an example, the smoker who goes from an away-from preference to a towards preference – which is an obvious change necessary for most people to successfully stop smoking – they may experience a very uncomfortable reaction from those who they care about. Again, always check for ecology after a change has been made.

LESSONS LEARNED FROM RAPPORT EXERCISES

Don't forget that your NLP rapport skills are also a form of modeling. As you match and mirror someone who is performing as an expert in a field, your brain and body quickly begins taking on attributes of that other person. Try matching the posture and vocal attributes of a popular person such as an actor or political figure and then see how the process makes you feel. Therefore, I am never amazed by actors who consistently play a certain role. Years later when you see them in an off-screen interview it is easy to see how the attributes have slowly become part of their personality. A great example of this is William Shatner, who always acted much like Star Trek's Captain Kirk decades after he stopped being filmed in the role.

IMPROVING YOUR OBSERVATIONAL SKILLS

Your ability to use NLP skills to successfully install new attributes in another person or organization rests entirely on developing superior abilities to calibrate. Medical doctors and PhD-level psychologists spend years developing such skills and continue perfecting them throughout their careers. During the two full years of my formal NLP training, I went from being totally overwhelmed and daunted by complexity of the various skills I was learning, to internalizing them to the point that they seemed natural. (Again, this is not a skill that you will be able to adequately develop during a quickie, comprehensive 10-day Practitioner or Master Practitioner program.) By constantly practicing with clients and patients, while sitting on a bench in the mall, while watching TV, in church, or at other times during the day, you will find that your skill will steadily increase.

DEMONSTRATION

I want to demonstrate how to calibrate to a subject's Eye Accessing Cues. For this demonstration you will need something to write with and to write on. When you are ready you may proceed.

On your paper draw a circle or simple face. On the left and right of the circle or face, draw six short horizontal lines. Two lines should be to the top left and right, two at the middle level both on the left and right, and the final two should be lower on the left and right. These six lines will represent times when your subject is looking up to your left or right, level to your left or right, and down to your left or right.

Next, I want to ask several questions. I am going to use the same questions presented above.

What was the color of your first car? Notice the eye movement of your subject. It will most likely up to the right or left. Typically, it will be to your right. Place a check mark on your diagram indicating your subject's

Visual Recall accessing direction.

What will be the color of your next home? On your diagram mark the direction that your subject looked. This will indicate their Visual Construct accessing.

What is the first sentence of your favorite song? Mark the direction that their eyes quickly shifted to. This is an indication of their Auditory Recall accessing.

What will be the first thing that you will say to your significant other during your next conversation? The direction that they look is an indicator of their Auditory Construct accessing.

How did you feel that last time someone gave you extremely good news? The direction that they looked is an indication of their Kinesthetic accessing. The remaining position of your diagram represents their Auditory Digital accessing.

At this point you have calibrated to your subject's eye accessing strategy.

ABOUT THE AUTHOR

This series is by Tim Brunson, who holds both Doctor of Clinical Hypnotherapy and Doctor of Philosophy Clinical Hypnotherapy degrees, has practiced hypnotherapy for 29 years with clients and patients referred to him by medical and mental health practitioners, has trained clinicians internationally, and has almost 3,000 hours of training much of which was medical and mental health related. Many of his courses are already available through Amazon in either short-read or longer books.

RESOURCES

General:

The International Hypnosis Research Institute

IHRI membership

Advanced-Neuro-Noetic-Hypnosis

Courses

Books, E-Books, And Audiobooks:

Sets

Elman Hypnotherapy: Beyond the Basics

Improving Your Performance Genius

Enhancing Performance: Unleashing Your True Potential (Bundled)

Innovations in Mind/Body Therapies

The Mind/Body Connection

The New Biology

The Neurology of Mind/Body Health

Transformation Revisited

The Immune System Primer

Using Imagery to Heal

A Quick Pain Management Primer

Healing the Body Basics

The Mind, Surgery, and Recovery

Calming Your Gut

Innovations in Mind/Body Therapies (Bundled)

The Neurology of Suggestion Series

The Neurology of Suggestion

Advanced Hypnotherapy Protocols and Applications

The Neurology of Suggestion Series (Bundled)

The Neurology of Suggestion Basics

Change: A New Paradigm for Transformation

Brain Potential: Enhancing and Inhibiting for Peak Performance

Reshaping: Changing your Brain and Body

Mastering Change: 10 Principles for Transformation

Achieving Lasting Change: A System for Transformation

Neurology of Suggestion Applications

The Neurology of Suggestion Basics (Bundled)

Neuro Linguistic Programming Basics

Mastering the NLP Communication Model

Developing Instant Rapport

The Basis of NLP Techniques

Modeling Behavior

Practical NLP Applications

Neuro Linguistic Programming Basics (Bundled)

Individual Books

Advanced Hypnotherapy Script Writing Techniques

Clinical Hypnotherapy Fundamentals

Healing the Body

Healing the Mind

New Directions in Hypnotherapy

Rapid Change: The Secrets of Lasting Personal and Group Transformation

Space/Time-based Interventions: Simple techniques that enhance hypnotherapy.